Usborne
First Sticker Book
Trains

Illustrated by
Annalisa Sanmartino
& Giulia Torelli

Contents

There are lots of stickers at the back
of this book for you to stick on each page.

Words by Sam Taplin
Designed by Matt Durber

At the station

It's the start of the day and the station is about to get busy. Stick on a train that's arriving, and fill the platform with people.

Double-decker trains

In some parts of the world there are double-decker (or bi-level) trains. Add some trains to the picture, and put more boats on the water.

Steam trains

People come here for a trip on an old-fashioned steam train.
Stick the rest of the trains onto the tracks.

The Flying Arrow

Underground trains

Beneath the bustling city, underground trains rumble through tunnels. Add the trains to the picture.

WAY OUT

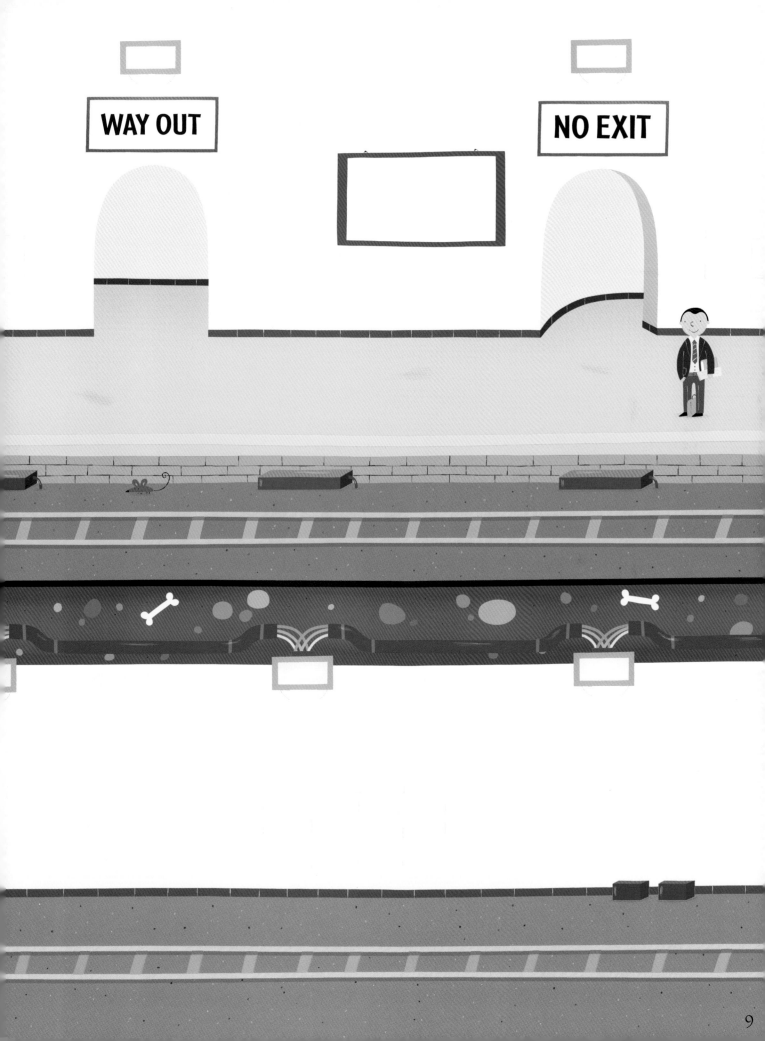

WAY OUT

NO EXIT

Monorail

Monorail trains glide smoothly through this city on tracks high above the traffic. Stick a train on the track, and cars on the road.

Shiny Shoe Shop

BILL'S BAKERY

Freight trains

Freight trains carry big, heavy containers
full of everything from car engines to food.
Add some containers to these trains.

54321

FREIGHT

0246

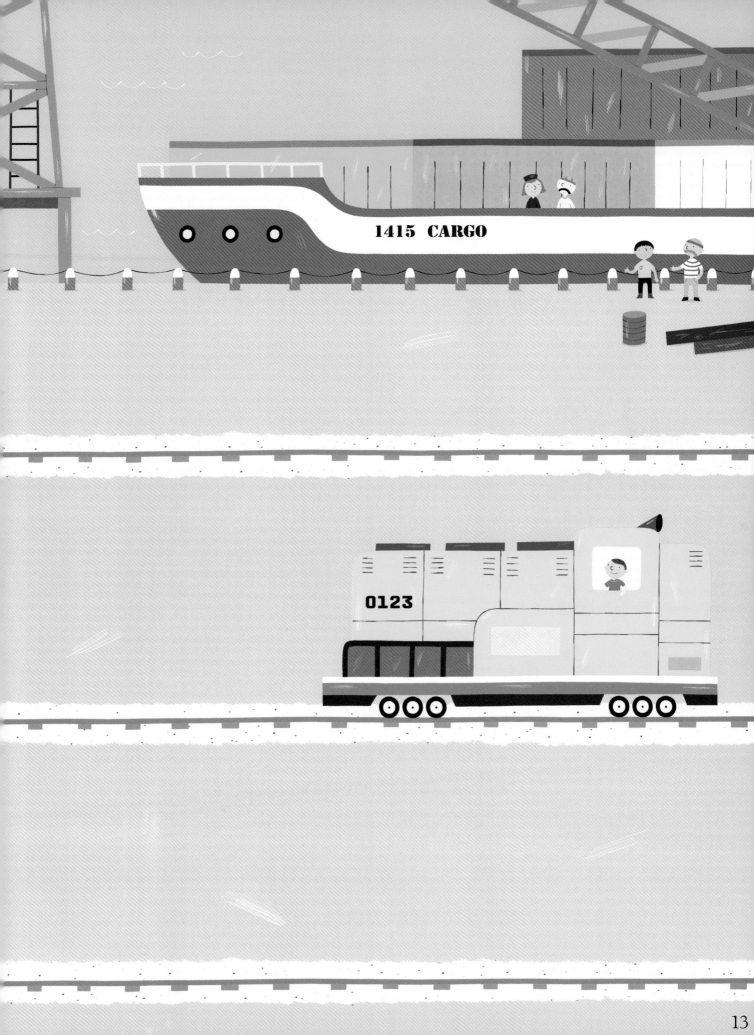

Rolling highways

Rolling highways are enormous trains that carry
trucks through the mountains of Europe.
Add the trains and trucks to these tracks.

Build the steam engine

Use the stickers to make your own steam engine.

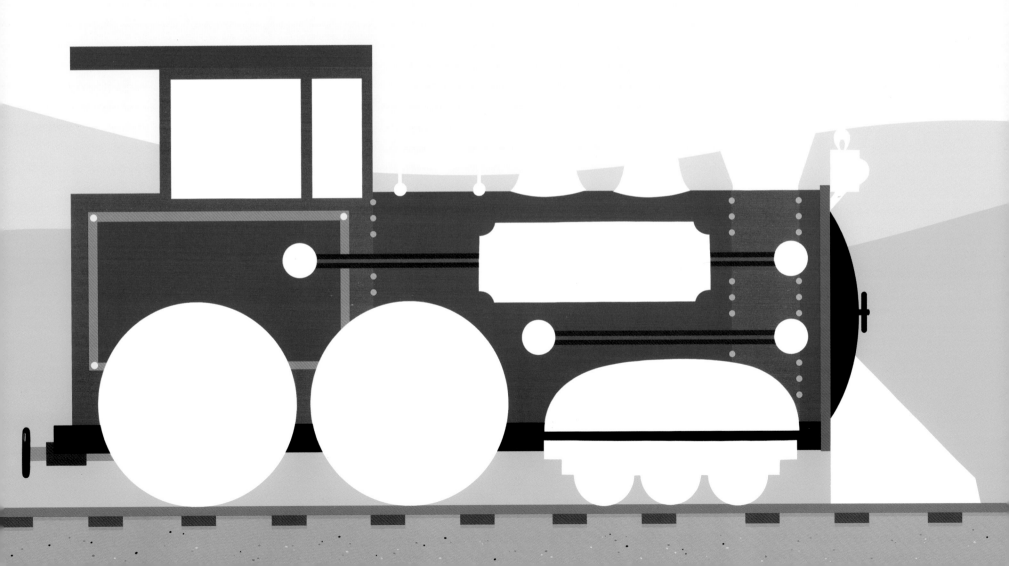

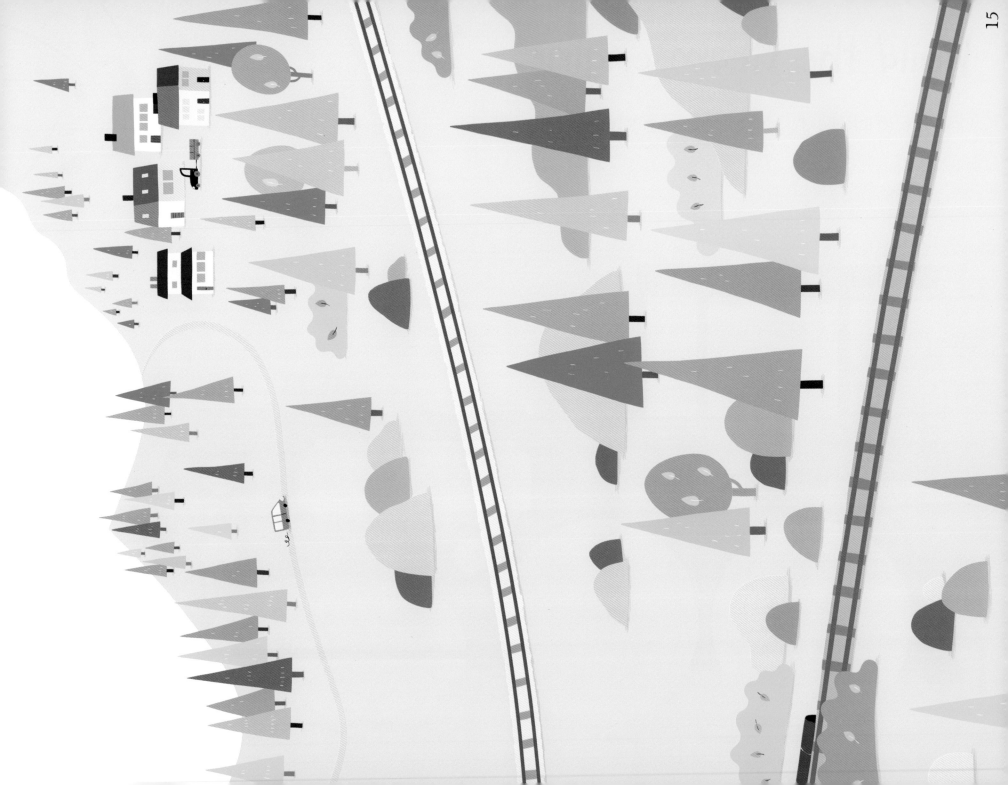